The

Nine Principles of Agile Planning

CREATE NIMBLE AND DYNAMIC FORECASTING IN YOUR ORGANIZATION.

David S. Pabst, CPA/CITP

To the many CFOs, Finance teams, and business leaders creating forecasting processes to help their organizations grow. This book is born from the fire of many planning and forecasting projects to help new souls avoid the pitfalls of failed forecasting projects and instead create long-lasting, dynamic, and nimble forecasting engines that will provide enduring positive change for your organizations.

CONTENTS

THE NINE PRINCIPLES OF AGILE PLANNING

FOCUS ON THE IMPORTANT THINGS

PLAN REAL-WORLD INITIATIVES

DERIVE FINANCIAL FORECASTS FROM REAL-WORLD PLANS

ALIGN PLANS TO LONG-TERM GOALS

ASSESS MULTIPLE OUTCOMES & SCENARIOS

MAKE PLANS EASY TO UPDATE

MANY SMALL PLANS ARE BETTER THAN 1 BIG PLAN

DETAIL != ACCURACY

THE WORLD KEEPS CHANGING – CHANGE WITH IT!

A BETTER WAY TO FORECAST

Your new planning, forecasting, and budgeting transformation project starts with excitement as you rally your leaders, team members, and internal customers around a new and better way to budget and forecast. You find other leaders to join you on your quest to improve the organization. You assemble a project team to figure out the best way to forecast everything from revenues (sales), expenses, headcount, capital investments, and every other aspect of the organization. Your forecasting project starts!

Creating a new planning and forecasting process is an opportunity that comes around once in a decade. You need to get it right.

This opportunity comes with great responsibility. You need to lead others in the right way to plan and forecast—a way that will be nimble and fast. A way that will be embraced for the information it produces, and one that allows the process to sense changes in the operating environment faster than ever.

Use this chance to develop an Agile Planning philosophy that encourages rapid development of plans, that can be quickly iterated, are easy to understand, and actionable. Take advantage of the golden age of cloud-based planning tools to facilitate these Agile Planning objectives.

I have seen organizations succeed in deploying a planning and forecasting process like this by balancing the many dimensions of planning. These successful organizations ensure that everyone on their team is educated and lives by a set of guiding principles. These guiding principles create a framework to determine which requirements to take on, and how to solve those requirements in ways that enhance the overall forecasting process.

On the other side, I have seen organizations spend millions of dollars to create new, bloated, and cumbersome planning processes that are worse than the preceding ones. These forecasting processes fail within a few years, and everyone goes back to forecasting in spreadsheets.

You need a forecasting and planning process that is easy to update, not too detailed, supported by automation, close to the people running the business, and aligned to long-term goals—one that can signal instantly when business conditions are starting to change.

Organizations with agile forecasting processes were able to detect and react to the COVID-19 pandemic when everything changed in a matter of weeks. Without a modern forecasting process, slower organizations could not respond until they saw their quarterly results. Were you able to take advantage of business opportunities during the pandemic, or did the pandemic blindside you?

You need a nimble, agile process that can adapt, iterate quickly, and help the organization manage itself in good and bad economic conditions.

The major software vendors want to sell you the promise of turnkey forecasting systems—Adaptive, Anaplan, OneStream, Oracle, Planful, and SAP provide modern, cloud-based planning suites. These tools are an effective method for constructing an Agile Planning process, but they are not an instant cure-all. You need to look at your goals through the lens of building an Agile Planning process and apply these cloud tools to get you there.

These new tools shine by enabling interconnected, collaborative, dynamic processes across teams with nearly infinite processing capacity provided at a nominal cost.

They will only be beneficial if you follow the *Nine Principles of Agile Planning.*

Who is this book for?

If you are a CFO, CIO, Finance manager, or Analyst embarking on a planning and forecasting redesign and about to implement a cloud-based process—use the *Nine Principles of Agile Planning* to give you a fighting chance for forecasting success. Use the *Nine Principles of Agile Planning* as a framework to meet your goals in a balanced way—focusing across nine different perspectives.

If you do not follow the Nine Principles you might be looking for a job once your organization realizes you have created a slow, low-value forecasting process. People living in your process will hate it and move onto something else to get their jobs done. Your forecasting process could fail!

Choose the alternative.

The Nine Principles will teach you how to build a process that reacts quickly and produces actionable information that helps run your business. Planners living in your process will love it because the process makes their lives easier. Your business partners will thank you for making it easier to run their parts of the organization. You will be a forecasting hero!

Embrace the *Nine Principles of Agile Planning*...

NINE PRINCIPLES

The Nine Principles of Agile Planning combine and reinforce each other, creating strength and durability. Use this strength to achieve nimble, dynamic, and evolving forecasts in a changing world.

The Nine Principles are:

1. Focus on the Important Things
2. Plan Real-World Initiatives
3. Derive Financial Forecasts from Real-World Plans
4. Align Plans to Long-Term Goals
5. Assess Multiple Scenarios and Outcomes
6. Make Plans Easy to Update
7. Many Small Plans are Better than One Big Plan
8. Detail Does Not Equal Accuracy
9. The World Keeps Changing—Change With It!

Principle #1: *Focus on the Important Things* invests your time and energy planning and forecasting the elements of your business that make a difference. Why spend time and energy forecasting the aspects of your business that are not material—or if they are material, are not controllable?

Many items in your business are fixed and recurring unless you make hard decisions to change them. Stop wasting time planning items like this unless you are going to change them by, for example, reducing headcount, moving your headquarters, or winding down a product or service.

Your process needs to forecast these ongoing items automatically, for example, growing your expenses with inflation.

When it is time to make the hard decision to bend a recurring, fixed part of your organization, Principle #2: *Plan Real-World Initiatives* can help. Initiative-building assigns people, time, and money to force a fixed, recurring item to change from its current activity level. Your process needs to incorporate real-world initiatives that can be executed, tracked, and measured throughout the year. An example of an initiative might be "cutting headquarters operating costs by 20% next year by installing new air conditioning."

Planning real-world initiatives gives your business leaders tangible to-do lists that are linked to the organization's financial forecasts.

Principle #3: *Derive Financial Forecasts from Real-World Plans* prevents you from building your financial projections in a vacuum. Too many organizations build their forecasts starting with their financial statements and work backward to figure out how to meet their forecasting targets. As an example, you might use a growth rate of 10% to project next year's Revenues (Sales). Instead, you should start by forecasting your operational activity levels, and then use these activity levels to derive your financial forecasts. There are many operational activity levels that are useful when driving your forecast, such as the number of deals, customers, quantities, units, hours, clicks, shipments, and so on.

Principle #4 reminds you to *Align Plans to Long-Term Goals* to think about the organization's long-term strategic objectives balanced with your near-term needs. Every action the organization takes in the present should be in support of its strategic goals. If the organization invests resources—time, money, and people—it needs to be in furtherance of the organization's long-term goals. A modern planning process will make it easy to align your near-term actions with your long-term goals.

Principle #5 helps you design a process to *Assess Multiple Scenarios and Outcomes.* None of us can reliably predict the future. Could you have predicted black swans such as COVID-19 or 9/11 during your annual budgeting process? You need a process that can evaluate downside risks and upside opportunities and not get hung up on one approved budget.

The fifth principle encourages your organization to build a series of plans, probabilities, and outcomes for what *could* happen. With a modern forecasting process, it can be easy to develop these alternative business scenarios by tagging which initiatives to accelerate if business picks up or adjusting your business activity levels if business slows down.

Principle #6: *Make Plans Easy to Update* encourages continuous evolution and iteration of your plans daily, weekly, and monthly. Too many organizations invest months trying to develop the perfect business plan, fighting internally over resources only to end up with an outdated plan. The process needs to be easy, simple, and efficient to encourage the continuous updating of business plans.

Principle #7: *Many Small Plans are Better than One Big Plan* subdivides the planning process when it becomes too complicated or time-consuming. When any part of your planning process becomes too big, with contributions from too many people, it will slow down and become less valuable. A quick update of a single area will take a long time when it needs to be coordinated with other stakeholders in the process.

Breaking a big forecasting process into smaller pieces gets the process closer to the managers in the business and improves the efficiency of the process.

On a macro level, having smaller, discrete forecasting processes makes your organization more flexible. As your business changes over time with acquisitions, divestitures, or the introduction of new products and services, you can easily add, modify, or shut down parts of the forecasting process.

Principle #8: *Detail Does Not Equal Accuracy* balances planning at an efficient level of detail while ensuring there is enough granularity to operate the business. Finding the right level of detail will lead to faster planning cycles and greater adoption. Too often, organizations attempt to forecast at the lowest level of available raw data—every product, customer, employee, and so on. Forecasting at an extreme level of detail is time-consuming and focuses people on the mechanics of the process versus managing the business.

Today's leading forecasting processes limit the amount of data a person needs to review. Behind the scenes your forecasting process can use more data than ever. You can use real-time data collected from across the organization to drive the forecasting process and build an early-warning system to alert you when trends start diverging from your forecasts.

Over the past few years, with the advent of the Internet of Things (IoT), your organization is collecting data from every customer, employee, process, and system. As you define a future forecasting process, you can tap into these real-time datasets. The trick is consuming raw IoT data in a way that can be quickly understood during a forecasting cycle without being overwhelming.

The final principle—*The World Keeps Changing—Change With It!*—is a reminder that your work is never done promoting, advocating, and evolving a planning process. A typical organization will spend a large amount of blood, sweat, and tears to implement a new process with a new software package. This is the beginning.

Your forecasting process is a living, breathing entity made of people, sub-processes, and systems. The organization is constantly changing, and your forecasting process needs to evolve with it. This requires a sustained investment in resources to support the process's evolution and relevance.

PRINCIPLE #1: FOCUS ON THE IMPORTANT THINGS

Principle #1: *Focus on the Important Things* avoids a forecasting process that treats everything equally. You should focus your forecasting process where it matters most and where there is an opportunity to change behavior. You need to apply your limited forecasting resources in areas where you can get a return on your time and effort.

THE 80/20 RULE

Italian economist Vilfredo Pareto recognized that 20% of the population owned 80% of land in nineteenth-century Italy.[1] His idea has been adapted for business and technology and is commonly known as the "Pareto Principle." The Pareto Principle can be applied to financial forecasting—for example, focusing on the 20% of your customers that account for 80% of your Revenue. Or reverse it to ensure you construct a forecasting process that avoids spending too much effort on the 80% of items that make up 20% of your results.

As you design a planning and forecasting process, focus your organization's energy on the areas of the business that will make a difference in your operations. Do not treat all of your revenues and expenses equally during planning. This is an inefficient use of your resources. Alternatively, evaluate which items are material to the organization and which items, if actively managed, could change the organization's direction.

---

[1] Kevin Kruse. "The 80/20 Rule And How It Can Change Your Life," Forbes, March 7, 2016, www.forbes.com/sites/kevinkruse/2016/03/07/80-20-rule/?sh=5da4aa203814.

ARE YOU FOCUSED ON THE WRONG THINGS?

You need to take a step back and ask: Are we planning too many data points? Do we ask our forecasters to plan every possible item?

One Fortune 100 company cripples its labor and headcount forecasting process by using too much detail. Their two hundred analysts review every single name and salary across the organization's 50,000 employees every month!

As the month starts, analysts commence forecasting by printing out the employee roster. They compare the employee list against their previous forecast to identify unexpected hires, terminations, and transfers.

It takes each analyst a whole day to reconcile their part of the employee list and build a new forecast. When you add up all of this time across 200 people, their forecast consumes 1,600 hours of effort! This is a significant investment of resources.

Another area where organizations struggle is spending too much time forecasting their fixed and recurring line items that are unlikely to change. Items like Rent, Maintenance, and Repairs. Even items that people think are variable expenses are often fixed. As an example, Salary Expenses are generally a fixed cost unless you are planning a big layoff.

If you are not trying to bend the cost curve for these and other recurring items, do not spend time forecasting them.

A third example of using too much detail occurs when Finance tries to forecast every new purchase. Finance creates a spreadsheet listing each purchase that will be made over the next year, noting when each purchase will be made, its useful life, and its salvage value. Do you really need to know how many desks or laptops you are buying next year?

A fourth signal that you may not be prioritizing your forecasting efforts: does your forecast look like your general ledger?

Many planning processes start by mimicking the accounting system. This is a fast way to get started and can give you a financial framework for developing a forecast, but the Chart of Accounts is meant to meet external reporting, tax, and regulatory needs. It is not designed to answer questions like which products you should sell, which customers to target, or which investments to make. If you see your organization forecasting by accounts, departments, legal entities, intercompany segments, and other accounting fields, take a step back and assess whether this leads you down a path of planning too many items.

When you forecast too many areas in extreme detail like in these examples, it eats up precious time and resources. You need to focus on items that matter and spend less effort on the other items. Try to focus on the 20% of the items that account for 80% of the results.

WHAT CAN YOU DO?

Print out your P&L and Balance Sheet!

We will identify which items are fixed versus variable and which items have a high versus low impact on your organization.

Review and determine if each major line item on your P&L is fixed or variable in nature. Fixed items usually stay flat and do not vary much over time. Variable items adjust with business activity levels, slowing and accelerating with the business's ebb and flow.

Second, for each item determine its materiality. High materiality items are the ones that determine your organization's success. Less strategic items have a low materiality.

Do this for each item: Revenues (Sales), Returns, Allowances, Costs of Goods, and common expenses like Travel, Telephone, and Taxes. Repeat this process for each item on your Balance Sheet, including Cash, Payables, Inventory, Investments, Fixed Assets, Receivables, Debt, and so on.

Ask yourself:

- If we plan it, will it influence how we run our business?
- Does anyone use the forecast for this item?
- How much time do we spend planning this line item?
- How many people are involved?
- How many times a year do we update it?
- Is forecasting this item valuable to the organization?

Once you have performed this assessment, group your items into a matrix like this (examples shown):

	Fixed	Variable
High Materiality	*Utilities Costs*	*Revenues (Sales) and Product Costs*
Low Materiality	*Telecom Expenses*	*IT projects*

When you have your major line items organized, apply the following guidelines to find the most efficient forecasting methodology for each type of item:

	Fixed	Variable
High Materiality	<ul><li>Automate.</li><li>Use trends such as an *average run rate* to forecast.</li><li>When effecting change, follow Principle #2: *Plan Real-World Initiatives.*</li></ul>	<ul><li>Highest focus.</li><li>Develop detailed, business area-specific plans.</li><li>Use Principle #7: *Many Smalls Plans are Better than One Big Plan.*</li></ul>

Low Materiality	• Automate. • Use trends such as an *average run rate* to forecast. • Minimize effort.	• Automate. • Develop forecast with volume-based measures like Shipments, Units, Employees, or Hours • Use Principle #3: *Derive Financial Forecasts from Real-World Plans.*

STRATEGIES FOR FIXED ITEMS

You need to spend minimal time and effort forecasting your fixed and recurring line items. Since you cannot control it, assume the trend continues. Use automation to update the forecasts for these line items.

A modern, cloud-based planning system can easily automate forecasts for these line items with little intervention from your team. When actual financial results get loaded, the system reforecasts the future based on preselected methodologies.

Planners love this. It reduces spreadsheet work and gives them the flexibility to select a planning methodology that works for them.

Common methods that you can select to automate your forecast for these line items include:

- Using last month's actuals.
- Using an average trend, like a 3-month rolling average.
- Drawing from a relationship with another financial line (e.g., Travel Expenses as a percentage of Revenues).
- Copying last year's actuals for the same period.

When it is time to bend one of these line items up or down, some-one in the organization will come to you with a proposal. If a business leader states, "We need to get rent under control" or "Telecom expenses are too high," ask them: "What projects should we take on to get them fixed?"

These proposals are initiatives, which are covered in Principle #2: *Plan Real-World Initiatives.* An initiative is a project, a time-boxed effort with a goal and an owner. The goal is to make a change. The owner is the business leader that will execute the initiative to achieve the goal.

Examples of initiatives that can bend a fixed item's trend are:

- Improving the energy efficiency of a building to reduce energy expenses.
- Searching for a lower-cost lease to reduce Rent Expenses.
- Introducing a product line to increase Revenues (Sales).
- Replacing outdated manufacturing equipment to reduce Cost of Goods Sold.

For items like this, you will continue to plan the fixed, recurring running costs using automation and then bend the existing activity level with a specific initiative.

As an added benefit, separating your fixed, ongoing costs from your initiatives provides visibility into what it takes to "run the business" independent from what it will take to "transform the business." Traditional forecasting approaches often co-mingle these two components.

Run	Transform
Trends	Initiatives
Fixed, recurring, trended forecasting – generally automated	Project-based Initiatives bend forecast for a fixed item up or down

STRATEGIES FOR VARIABLE ITEMS

You need to take a different approach for line items that change with business or economic activity, like Revenues (Sales) or Manufacturing Costs. Do not use trended run-rate based automated forecasts for these items. Instead, estimate business activity volumes and use these volumes to derive a financial forecast.

As an alternative to trending the financial measure itself (e.g., Revenues), you need to identify the underlying Volume and Rate. For an element like Revenues, the volume might be Quantity Sold, and the rate might be Selling Price. To revise the forecast for the underlying volume, use automated trends to project future activity, as we did with recurring and fixed items. Next, find the right person in your organization to update the corresponding rates, like price lists, material costs, or hourly rates.

The process will generate a financial forecast by multiplying Volume by Rate using the underlying Volume and Rate forecasts.

If an accurate forecast is not possible because more detail is needed, take a step back and ask a few questions. Are the right people forecasting these items? Does this process need to be delegated deeper within the organization? If so, it is time to break the forecasting for this line item into a smaller, more focused planning process.

Principle #7: *Many Small Plans are Better than One Big Plan* breaks a complicated process into a smaller and more focused forecast. These smaller forecasts get closer to the relevant business leaders and helps them run and manage their business while indirectly creating a financial forecast.

Examples of these smaller, modular plans include:

- Commission planning by Sales Rep
- Revenue forecasting by Client
- Production planning for a factory
- Marketing campaign planning
- Project planning for an IT organization

Many organizations take shortcuts forecasting items like this, using trends or Volume * Rate methodologies. If these methodologies cannot yield reliable results, you need to drive these planning processes deeper in the organization... closer to the true business owner.

FOCUS YOUR EFFORTS

For your low-value and recurring items, Principle #1: *Focus on the Important Things* teaches several strategies to sharpen your efforts, including using automation to trend your low-value recurring items. Principle #2: *Plan Real-World Initiatives* builds upon this by teaching you how to use initiatives to bend your fixed items. Principle #3: *Derive Financial Forecasts from Real-World Plans* teaches you how to forecast the parts of your business that speed up or slow down as business activity levels change. Principle #7: *Many Small Plans are Better Than One Big Plan* moves operational planning away from Finance and closer to the managers running the organization. Finally, when we get to Principle #9: *The World Keeps Changing—Change With It!* as your organization evolves, an item that might be fixed and recurring now might grow in its importance over time and will need its methodology adjusted.

The Nine Principles work together, focusing your forecasting on the 20% that makes a difference and not the distracting 80%.

PRINCIPLE #2:
PLAN REAL-WORLD
INITIATIVES

When you *Plan Real-World Initiatives,* you bridge the gap between actions in real life and how those actions can bend the revenue or expense trends for your fixed and recurring items. As we walked through in Principle #1: *Focus on the Important Things*, you should not spend effort forecasting your recurring items unless you are ready to do something about it. Initiatives are that "something."

Initiatives are projects that adjust your existing trends. An initiative might be used by the Vice President of Marketing to try to boost Revenues (Sales) on a stagnating product. Or, the Facilities Manager may want to save energy costs by installing new air conditioning systems. Without an initiative to bend Revenues or Expenses, those items move along at their current activity level.

What are the qualities of an initiative?

- Initiatives are additive to the current run rate.
- Initiatives bend the revenue or expense curve of one or more P&L line items up or down.
- Initiatives are investments of people, money, or time.
- Initiatives are projects that need to be managed. These projects have a life: a beginning, middle, and end.
- Initiatives have owners and teams to execute them.
- Initiatives are aligned to strategic goals and objectives.

WHY SHOULD WE PLAN BY INITIATIVE?

Does your organization have two separate forecasting processes?

Does Finance run your financial forecasting process? Is there a second process run by your corporate functions like IT, Legal, Marketing, or R&D? Are these functions soliciting requests for what their groups should work on? Do their project lists integrate into the financial forecasting process?

When different groups create their own project request and prioritization systems, the organization's risks increase. Leadership loses centralized visibility on what the organization is doing. Finance is hard-pressed to act in its stewardship role to protect the organization, and it is difficult for Finance to develop a consolidated financial outlook incorporating everyone's proposed internal projects.

Without a centralized view of the work in the organization, unapproved, shadow skunk-works projects are widespread. Different parts of the organization could be working on competing projects, and managers may be approving their own pet projects.

These shadow projects can lead to a variety of organizational risks, such as:

1. Internal teams get spread thin because they are working on too many competing projects.
2. Projects take longer and need more funding than expected as stakeholders were skipped when developing cost estimates. Department managers might launch projects thinking they can do it alone, and they do not factor in input from supporting teams like IT or Facilities.
3. Resources could have been used on higher-value projects elsewhere in the organization.
4. The organization might not achieve long-term strategic goals because teams are working on the wrong priorities, as we will see in Principle #4: *Align Plans to Long-Term Goals.*

It gets worse if your organization distributes budgets in a top-down fashion, giving each area an annual budget. Managers think they own their top-down budgets. It takes away from accountability and transparency if different areas do not need to collaborate and agree on which projects move forward.

In organizations using top-down funding, you might see your CEO, CFO, and business leaders getting nervous. Does your CFO ask questions like:

- Why is there no budget to do a [...]? We approved a lot of money this year.
- Why are my priorities always late?
- What is everyone working on?
- Why are we not achieving our organizational goals?
- Why are projects always over budget?
- What is Marketing (or IT or Legal or R&D or any other department) doing?
- Why are we doing similar projects in two different parts of the organization?

If this sounds like your organization, you can fix it with Principle #2.

HOW DO WE FIX THIS?

You need to create a forecasting cycle that captures proposed business initiatives with a process to adjudicate which ones to take on. Most organizations create an investment steering committee to decide which initiatives to approve, making sure that the organization is aligned to complete them.

Initiatives are proposed projects with a financial impact, such as:

- Investments in research and development.
- Marketing and advertising campaigns (e.g., spend resources with online, radio, or tv media)
- Investments to reduce operating expenses: new equipment, solar panels, or employee safety training.
- Capital initiatives that invest in the organization's future, like IT systems or Facilities projects

- Hybrid projects that have elements of operating, efficiency, and capital initiatives, like new product introductions. These will have a long-term operating impact with new revenues, costs, and capital investments.

INTEGRATE WITH OTHER GOAL-SETTING METHODOLOGIES

To turbo-charge initiative planning, you can link up with your organization's other goal-setting processes. Linking goal setting with initiative planning can help the organization decide which projects to take on.

Many initiatives are great ideas.

You need to find the right mix of short, medium, and long-term wins while limiting the number of in-flight initiatives. Your organization can only execute a limited set of projects simultaneously before you exceed your internal capacity. If you take on too many initiatives, nothing will get done. You need to make sure competing needs do not constrain the initiatives you formally authorize.

When you set up your initiative cycle, you will get ideas from across the organization. You will need a prioritization process that can approve small items and escalate larger ones. This will require defining multiple prioritization levels. In the first round of prioritization, Managers and Directors can prioritize items for their areas. As proposed initiatives get bigger, higher levels of authority will need to collaborate to approve items.

To help the prioritization process, all proposed initiatives should be categorized from both quantitative and qualitative perspectives.

On the quantitative side, you will want to look at your proposed initiative portfolio by financial return measures like internal rate of return, net present value, payback period, or discounted cash flows. These are great for tie-breaking two or more strategic initiatives with similar qualitative and strategic benefits.

Looking at the qualitative aspects of your proposed initiatives ensures that you balance financial goals with your non-financial goals simultaneously. Even non-financial qualitative goals have second-order financial effects, like "improving employee wellness" or "increasing training"—these might reduce costs or increase retention, but they can be hard to quantify.

To help find this balance between quantitative and qualitative prioritization, consider using a goal-setting framework with your initiative planning, for example:

- Balanced Scorecard
- Objectives & Key Results (OKRs)
- Strategic Goals
- Master Plans and Roadmaps (for Facilities or IT)

Balanced Scorecard

The Balanced Scorecard sets and monitors goals across four categories: financial, customer, internal, and innovation. Within each dimension, a set of measures track progress over time.

When an initiative is proposed, the submitter articulates how their proposed investment will improve one or more measures in at least one of the four quadrants. An organization should avoid initiatives that do not support one of the four areas.

Objectives & Key Results

OKRs are a modern goal-setting process. Objectives are the destinations you would like to get to, such as "increasing revenues over the next six months," and Key Results are the steps you are going to take to make it happen...also known as Initiatives!

For example:

- Build out the Sales team by hiring 5 new Sales Reps and increase next quarter's Revenues (Sales) by 25%.
- Reduce our Selling Price by $5 a unit by switching to a new raw material vendor.

- Start a new Facebook marketing campaign to improve sales leads by 20%.

Initiative planning and OKRs naturally align by bridging financial forecasting with actionable operational plans your leaders can execute against.

Strategic Goal Setting

A CEO sets Strategic Goals to get employees marching toward a vision of where the organization needs to be several years in the future. Usually, there are a limited number of these goals, typically five to ten. These goals do not change often and remain stable for several years.

Examples of Strategic Goals are:

- Improve the customer experience by investing in first-class mobile experiences.
- Eliminate all retail locations – go all-in online.
- Eliminate all datacenters by moving to software-as-a-service.

When initiatives are suggested, they need to be considered in the context of how they advance the organization's Strategic Goals. To do this, during the initiative submission process, ask the submitter how their initiative supports a Strategic Goal. If an initiative supports multiple goals, ask the submitter to determine percentages of how their proposed initiative proportionally addresses each Strategic Goal.

As these proposed initiatives move up the approval process, the organization should only approve initiatives that align with their Strategic Goals.

Master Planning and Roadmaps

Organizations with large campuses, such as universities, hospitals, and airports, often conduct strategic reviews to evaluate where their customer volumes are headed over the next 5-10 years.

An airport, university, or hospital will study the region and look at whether people and businesses are moving into the market. Based on those trends, they will determine how they need to re-configure their facilities to meet upcoming demand. These studies develop into a master plan of projects, big projects like reconfiguring terminals, building parking garages, and so on.

These long-term projects are initiatives!

HOW DO I PROPOSE AN INITIATIVE?

Create a proposal intake form and set up a centralized initiative tracking log. Technology can make this easy by removing the manual administration and getting everyone's information into a common database.

Your proposal intake form should capture the following items:

- Sponsors, justification, and business case
- Required financial investment—what is it going to cost for salaries, contractors, equipment, and capital?
- Funding sources—how are we going to pay for this project? Can we pay from operations? Do we need to borrow? Fund-raise?
- Operating impacts—how does this initiative overlay on the financial forecast? Which line items on the P&L and Balance Sheet are impacted by this project?
- Qualitative benefits—how does this initiative support our short, medium, and long-term goals?
- Capital asset information—if this project involves purchasing or building capital assets, how will the newly acquired assets impact our Balance Sheet and Cash Flow?
- Stakeholder impact assessment—who else needs to provide resources or weigh in on this item? IT, Facilities, Purchasing, Marketing, Legal, Manufacturing, and Sales should weigh in on initiatives.

TECHNOLOGY MAKES INITIATIVES EASY!

Modern planning tools make it easy to capture and prioritize initiatives. Everyone in the organization knows where to go to propose a new internal initiative, and automated workflow will route a proposed initiative to the right place.

You may want to set up working areas where managers can develop their own investment roadmaps. These private sandboxes allow managers to think strategically about their upcoming needs. Encourage managers to use these sandboxes, as the organization benefits when managers think a few steps ahead about what they need to do in their areas to be successful.

Managers can work their list, change priorities, and add details. They can add items they know are coming, such as equipment replacements, technology upgrades, and building renovations. They can add ideas even if they are just exploratory.

When it is time to ask for approval on an initiative, managers can take an item from their roadmap and start the approval cycle. If the initiative gets approved, their initiative layers on top of the baseline financial forecast discussed in Principle #1: *Focus on the Important Things.* This bends their forecast up or down from their previous trend.

From Finance's bird's-eye view, you can see emerging needs across the organization. You can spot synergies where two parts of the organization are trying to do similar things. You can promote projects that will make a difference.

When you use a system to manage this process, the financial forecast can update in real-time as initiatives evolve. If the size and scale of an initiative adjusts, these changes ripple into the financial forecast. If an initiative gets approved, declined, or put on hold, you can see these events reflected in the forecast as well.

As the planning process concludes, each manager in the organization can see a list of approved initiatives that they need to execute in the upcoming year. Higher managerial levels can see all the approved initiatives across their sphere of influence. And, supporting cross-functional groups like IT, HR, Legal, Facilities, and Purchasing can see how they will need to support the broader organization's priorities.

As the year progresses executing in-flight initiatives, your initiative planning system continuously monitors progress. Your project management teams can use the system to manage execution and request additional resources. Accounting can identify initiatives that are wrapping-up and place any new assets into service.

INITIATIVES BEND CURVES

Initiatives are forecasting's secret weapons. Initiatives are actionable projects that increase revenues, decrease costs, or have other financial impacts. Initiatives are powerful tools that "transform" the fixed and recurring aspects of your business.

Make it easy to enter, prioritize, and adjudicate initiatives using a centralized system. Encourage your business leaders to think strategically by building their own initiative roadmaps. Align your initiative planning process with your other goal-setting methodologies.

Use forecasting's secret weapon: initiatives.

PRINCIPLE #3:
DERIVE FINANCIAL
FORECASTS FROM
REAL-WORLD PLANS

Is Finance building the financial forecast before consulting front-line business teams and corporate functions?

Are you forecasting your variable items using the same methodology as your fixed and recurring items?

If so, Principle #3 can help!

Most Finance folks think in financial terms—Revenues, Expenses, Assets, and Liabilities. They build their forecasts around a financial perspective: add a few percent to Revenue (Sales) or reduce Expenses by a few percent. When your organization starts and ends financial forecasting around a P&L and Balance Sheet, you run the risk of having a forecasting process that is divorced from the realities of the business.

You need to get the customer-facing parts of your business that build and sell things to be the focus. You need to leverage their insights and use their data.

To do this, you will need to build relationships across the organization. You will have to sit down with each area and learn their inputs, outputs, and costs. These experts know when the business is slowing down or speeding up, long before Finance figures it out. With their insights and data, you can collaborate to develop a forecasting methodology for the parts of your business that vary with activity, like Revenues (Sales).

It can be an excellent investment.

Finance gets an intelligent, dynamic financial forecast linked to what is happening on the frontlines. Operational teams get a process that can help run their organizations.

An integrated process like this can act as an early-warning system. It can watch, looking for when an operational volume forecast starts diverging from real-time data. Operational teams can react right away instead of waiting weeks for financial results to come in.

Principle #3 guides you through the process of linking the variable and material elements of your financial statements to your business's operational volumes. As we discussed in Principle #1, these volumes need to be paired to rates, such as prices and costs, to derive a financial forecast. By forecasting with volumes and rates unique to each area, your operational teams get tangible targets they can use to manage and measure their day-to-day operations.

DO NOT TREND VARIABLE ITEMS

In this fast-changing world, you cannot wait until you receive the final financial results from last month or last quarter. This information takes weeks to prepare, and by the time you use it in your forecast, it is already out-of-date; business activity might have already shifted.

If you see your organization using actual financial results as the driver to forecast variable items like Revenues or Costs by saying, "We think sales are going to increase 10% next year," this is a red flag that your organization is taking a shortcut.

Ask yourself: Where did this assumption come from? Is it based on the desire for upper management to meet external expectations? Is it based on the expected real-world activity level of the underlying business? How old is this data being used?

Trends should only be used to forecast variable items when performing strategic analysis. For example, looking a few years into the future to understand what the company might look like with different levels of growth. We will dig into balancing these longer-term planning needs with Principle #4: *Align Plans to Long-Term Goals* and Principle #5: *Assess Multiple Scenarios and Outcomes*.

IDENTIFY WHAT MOVES YOUR BUSINESS

To put Principle #3: *Derive Financial Forecasts from Real-World Plans* into practice, identify the variable, volume-based parts of your business—items like Revenues (Sales), Labor Expenses, Marketing Expenses, or Manufacturing Costs.

For each item, identify the business leader that is responsible. Go meet them. Get to understand how their function works. Ask them to explain their inputs, how their function produces value, and their outputs. Ask how they measure these items.

Each one of their components has a corresponding financial impact, likely measured in minutes, hourly cost, machine time, unit cost, projects, work orders, phone calls, and so on. To determine the corresponding rate for each volume-based measure, like machine time or phone calls, you may have to dig to understand the direct and indirect costs within that area.

As you engage the organization's business leaders, you realize two benefits. First, many operational teams will be grateful to get Finance's expertise in developing a forecasting process that links their operational activities to the organization's financial success. You are providing them with a modern process they do not have today.

Second, these operational, business-driven sub-processes produce much more intelligent and accurate forecasts. Your operational teams know to the minute what their business activity levels are, and you can harness this to improve financial forecasts. These teams can predict and forecast their volumes and changes to their costs much better than Finance.

As the world gets more and more connected, most operational measures are collected in real-time: orders submitted, materials purchased, items produced, employees hired, advertising clicks, and so on.

Your operational teams can provide access to real-time data and get this data into the forecasting process. As the business teams start to forecast their expected business volumes, the process can sound the alarm right away if real life begins to act strangely. Operational managers love being alerted that something is trending off from the forecast in real-time versus waiting weeks or months to see the financial results—when it is too late to react.

In the last few years, software-as-a-service solutions have flourished across every function in business. Most teams subscribe to niche solutions for their part of the business instead of building a spreadsheet or a custom application. These tools have permeated throughout organizations.

Legal uses a product to manage lawsuits and law firm billing. Treasury uses a cash management tool that downloads bank statements. Facilities uses a facility management platform with visibility into building energy and maintenance costs. IT uses a project management and time-tracking tool with insight into cost-to-serve and labor. Manufacturing uses an enterprise resource planning (ERP) platform to manage production with visibility into production costs and raw materials. HR uses a recruiting tool with insight into salaries, bonuses, and the supply of labor in the organization.

These systems are your sources for operational volumes and rates.

BUSINESS LEVERS ADD VALUE

Principle #3: *Derive Financial Forecasts from Real-World Plans* links real-world business activity levels to inform your financial forecasts. As the organization speeds up or slows down, your quantities, units, hours, and other volumes change to compensate. Using these real-world activity levels dramatically improves the accuracy and value of a financial forecast while simultaneously guiding your frontline business leaders.

As we integrate operational data to assist with managing the high-impact, variable parts of the business, we also need to remain faithful to the other Principles. Principle #8: *Detail Does Not Equal Accuracy* ensures that we balance using operational data without creating a too granular process. Principle #6 reminds us that whatever we do, a plan needs to be easy to update. If we cannot hold true to all these competing principles, sometimes we must break a big process into smaller ones by following Principle #7: *Many Small Plans are Better than One Big Plan.*

PRINCIPLE #4:
ALIGN PLANS TO
LONG-TERM GOALS

Forecasting is about the future, but too many organizations only think a few months ahead, leaving them without a map for where they need to go. When creating your agile forecasting process, you need to balance the Principles and make sure your short-term outlook blends with your organization's long-term goals in the years ahead.

The Principles we have covered so far focus on the present: planning what you can manage, deriving forecasts from real-world plans, and building initiatives. Principle #4 balances managing your business in the present with your longer-term goals.

ARE WE SHORT-TERM FOCUSED?

While staying focused on current operations is an essential part of forecasting, we need to make sure the organization also keeps an eye on the future.

I like to ask Finance teams if they have a process to support their CEOs and CFOs when they need to evaluate strategic options—their "big-bets." Most organizations evaluate strategic opportunities as they arise and do not have a standardized methodology to handle these requests.

If your organization can set up a formal process to think about long-term opportunities, you can increase the velocity at which you can react when your CEO and CFO need your help. You can react quickly when a new opportunity arises and provide analysis on how the opportunity will impact the organization's liquidity and financial health.

Most big events, like an acquisition or building a new facility, have complex interactions on the P&L, Balance Sheet, and Cash Flow that can be difficult to analyze quickly. You need to look at how to fund these events—by borrowing, issuing equity, or generating cash. You need to be able to model how the event will generate or consume cash and how the rest of the organization may need to provide resources in support.

With the proper process, Finance can help the organization propose and evaluate longer-term decisions and see how those big-picture decisions impact liquidity and financial health several years into the future.

WHERE TO START?

You need a standardized methodology to evaluate your "big-bets" separately from your core forecasting processes. These investments are large, ranging from new plants, facilities, campuses, and products. Generally, these items will have their own P&Ls, Balance Sheets, and Cash Flows.

Finance can use its expertise to help your CEO and CFO evaluate strategic options with an established and routine process. You should have the capability to evaluate a "big-bet" and be ready to go at a moment's notice. This avoids having a standard operating procedure that requires building new spreadsheets in an urgent situation. Your organization should be capable of evaluating these opportunities as they arise with a standardized process.

Some of the questions a strategic, long-term planning process can address include:

- How are cashflows impacted by this opportunity? How does it consume cash during its formative stage, and how does it then produce cash?
- What does the combined organization look like after the event?
- Are there cost savings that can be realized across the broader organization in the future?
- Do we need to borrow or issue stock to fund this?

- Will we break our debt covenants or other restrictions?
- What can we do with the cash we generate from the opportunity? Do we fund more investments, pay down debt, pay a dividend, or buy back stock?
- How do the non-cash elements impact our Balance Sheet and P&L, such as Amortization, Depreciation, and Goodwill?

HOW CAN WE INTEGRATE LONG-TERM THINKING?

You can improve your organization's ability to evaluate long-term strategic options by establishing a regular cadence to review its "big-bets" modeling methodology. This review process ensures the process is up to date and ready to go at a moment's notice. Finance can bring its significant modeling expertise and get different stakeholders—like Executives, Legal, or Treasury—to provide input.

Start by identifying organizational stakeholders that need to be part of this methodology review. Start with small, informal working sessions to get the organization used to dreaming about the future. Get this team thinking about evaluating "big-bets" and determining the key elements that need evaluation when "big-bets" arise.

Appoint someone to be the "big bets" modeler.

Make sure to provide this modeler with the right tools to be able to model these "big bets." You want to model them quickly and accurately without cumbersome and error-prone spreadsheets. You can provide this capability with the latest planning tools.

USE TECHNOLOGY

The newest cloud strategic modeling tools allow you to model changes to your existing business. You can integrate your existing financial run rate from your core reporting and forecasting systems and then layer on major structural changes. Strategic modeling tools combine the current state with the proposed change, so you can see how the combined organization will look several years in the future.

Your CEO or CFO can propose a "big-bet"—an acquisition, selling a business, or building a new business. You can develop multiple scenarios on how to fund these projects and see how they impact the overall enterprise. You can create a range of scenarios quickly and provide options to your business leaders about what the organization's financials will look like, depending on which options they choose.

These tools automate the linkages across your financial statements. For example, they are intelligent about allocating cash generated from your businesses. If your "big-bets" generate cash, you can evaluate paying down debt, issuing dividends, or buying back stock.

As you look to the future with your "big-bets," most long-range planning tools allow you to study multiple outcomes. You can run thousands of automated simulations to provide you with the best- and worst-case outcomes while assessing success probabilities.

One more way these modern strategic modeling tools provide value is their ability to seek an answer starting from your final result, like Earnings Per Share, and working backwards through your financial statements. You can selectively hold items on your Balance Sheet or P&L constant and see how other elements, like Revenues (Sales), would need to change to achieve the desired goal.

PLAY THE LONG GAME

Principle #4 plays the long game and prepares the organization for when your CEO or CFO asks, "Should we make this big-bet?" Most organization's forecasting efforts focus on the next quarter or two, but you better make sure you can play the long game!

PRINCIPLE #5:
ASSESS MULTIPLE SCENARIOS AND OUTCOMES

No plan survives first contact with the enemy.

The real world likes to interfere, and most organizations have a bit of hubris believing that a single forecast is good enough to operate their business. A single forecast is inherently flawed, based on a single set of expected events.

Principle #5: *Assess Multiple Scenarios and Outcomes* ensures the organization has considered a range of possibilities, both good and bad, with reaction plans ready to go. A better way to forecast is to document the range of possibilities that might happen. You need to have a menu of contingencies ready to go if business speeds up or slows down from what is expected in your core business case.

If you believe that your best attempt at a forecast is imperfect, then you can implement a forecasting process that compensates for the imperfections of normal forecasting. The first step is to articulate the assumptions that went into developing the forecast. Document the assumptions on how your organization thinks the business cycle, economy, politics, or extreme weather could impact your business's activity.

If you can articulate these assumptions, you can create a response plan for the possibility that those assumptions do not hold. This is not all downside thinking; you also need to consider what to do if real life is better than expected.

Multi-business case forecasting is a risk identification and quantification process. You can build this risk assessment right into your planning cycle. As your stakeholders develop their forecasts, they need to document their assumptions, probability of success, and their upside and downside perspectives.

The other Agile Principles streamline the process of capturing your upside and downside perspectives:

Principle #2: *Plan Real-World Initiatives* helps you develop a set of initiatives to execute if things go as planned, another if things go worse, and a third if things go better.

Principle #3: *Derive Financial Forecasts from Real-World Plans* lets you define factors that adjust as business activity volumes change, like the number of Shipments. Planners estimate Shipments when they build their most-likely business case. But you can ask the follow-up question: If the economy grows slower, or you face increased competition, how would Shipments change? The answers to these questions are the basis for building upside and downside business scenarios.

HOW DO ORGANIZATIONS FAIL AT ANALYZING MULTIPLE SCENARIOS?

Most organizations spend their time coordinating and building their mostly-likely business case. Few are at the maturity level that, during their process, they ask, "What could go right?" and "What could go wrong?"

I like to ask my clients if they have a process to go back and assess their forecast accuracy. Many organizations never go back and see if their forecast is any good. Did you hit your forecast? If you missed it, do you go back and tighten up the process to make future forecasts more accurate?

The first place to look when evaluating forecast accuracy is to review the organization's monthly variance reports. A quick scan of these reports will show actual results measured against the forecast for each line item, like Revenues (Sales), Costs, Utilities, Rent, and Travel. If the actual versus forecast variances are sporadic and occur across different parts of the P&L, this is a sign that the organization is not capturing and planning for upside and downside risks in its forecasts.

Recurring variances in the same part of the P&L is a symptom that the forecasting methodology for the line item is wrong. For these types of variances, you need to apply Principle #1: *Focus on the Important Things* and use the right approach to forecast these items. You need to ask: Should this item be run-rate, volume, initiative, or sub-plan based?

When organizations do capture their upside and downside risks, variance reporting is not a culmination of random variances. Their variance reporting looks like a scatterplot with the actual result plotted against the available business cases. Instead of a random "miss," the scatterplot draws the discussion to the closest business case and facilitates a discussion of why actuals are trending toward a specific business case.

Instead of calling out a variance, such as "we missed last month," there is context to interpret the results. When you have multiple business scenarios, it takes the guesswork out of saying "we are doing great" or "things are looking pretty bad." These business scenarios are already developed, and the actual results will fall somewhere between the best, mid, and worst cases.

START BY BUILDING OFF-RAMPS

You can live Principle #5 by documenting the business assumptions that go into your core forecasting case in your existing forecasting process. Document how you expect the external and internal environments to react, and then measure those assumptions as part of your normal forecast-variance reporting process.

As an example, if your core forecast expects inflation of 2%, write it down. If inflation is 2%, many of your operating expenses should show a 2% increase in the absence of any new transformative initiatives.

You can take this a step further with likely, but infrequent business events. You should articulate your assumptions around supply disruptions, hurricanes, earthquakes, power outages, labor strikes, pandemics, and so on.

Documenting these likely internal and external factors allows the organization to prepare plans that can be acted upon if real life does not play out the way everyone thought it would. I like to call these plans your off-ramps—your best- and worst-case contingency plans. These off-ramps are ready to go if there is a crash on the proverbial forecast highway.

Once you document the assumptions and contingencies within your core forecast, you can develop additional business cases. In addition to your core business case, create two more: a best-case and a worst-case. You can always add more, but these are the two to start with.

During the forecasting cycle, ask your participants to identify the actions they would take if the pace of the business changes significantly. Examples are:

Worst Case	<ul><li>**Pause/cancel** specific initiatives</li><li>**Reduce** sales volumes</li><li>**Increase** input costs</li><li>**Reduce** controllable expenses</li></ul>
Most Likely	<ul><li>Expected business initiatives</li><li>Expected sales volumes</li><li>Expected input costs</li><li>Expected controllable expenses</li></ul>
Best Case	<ul><li>**Accelerate/start** specific initiatives</li><li>**Increase** sales volumes</li><li>**Reduce** input costs</li><li>**Increase** controllable expenses</li></ul>

STRATEGIES TO EVALUATE MULTIPLE OPTIONS

You need to balance and leverage the other Principles to support Principle #5: *Assess Multiple Scenarios and Outcomes.*

Focus on what you can control; apply the 80/20 rule of planning— spending time and effort on what is controllable—and let uncontrollable items be systemically planned. Most of your recurring, fixed items will not change if business activity levels change. Do not plan contingencies for low-risk, low materiality items.

When planning your key business activity levels—Units, Shipments, People, Hours, and so on—ask your stakeholders to plan upside and downside volumes and rates. To simplify the process, ask them to submit scaling factors, like increasing volumes by 10% for upside and decreasing volumes by 20% for downside. Scaling factors are easier to work with than developing specific volumes for each business case. Scaling factors allow automated generation of your other business cases by mathematically applying the factors to your most-likely scenario volumes.

On the initiative side, ask your planners to think about what they would do if business speeds up or slows down. Ask which initiatives from their most-likely business scenario they would be forced to start, stop, or accelerate.

In parallel, document the external business assumptions that have gone into your most-likely forecast scenario. These can be reviewed as part of your monthly or quarterly business reviews to assess changes to your forecasts moving forward. Having discussions about these items can drive decisions about whether adjustments need to be made in your best, most-likely, or downside business scenarios.

You should also consider capturing the organization's assessment about external factors, such as:

Competition	<ul><li>New products</li><li>Pricing pressure</li><li>Counterfeiting/Piracy</li></ul>
Economy	<ul><li>Economic shock</li><li>Recession</li><li>Recovery</li></ul>
Compliance & Regulatory	<ul><li>New regulations</li><li>New laws</li></ul>
Supply Chain	<ul><li>Supply disruptions</li><li>Manufacturing capacity</li><li>Distribution issues</li><li>Third-party outsourcing</li></ul>
Labor Availability	<ul><li>Labor supply</li><li>Labor pricing</li></ul>
Financial	<ul><li>Interest rates</li><li>Ability to issue stock</li></ul>

For these external factors, it can be helpful to document a limited number of events and apply them to your best, most-likely, and worst-case scenarios.

To quantify how they should be layered into your financial forecasts, ask these questions:

- What is the likelihood of this event occurring?
- What is the financial impact or the impact on business volumes if this happens?
- What actions would we take if the risk occurs?

Typically, you can balance risks in your forecasts by multiplying the likelihood by the financial impact. You can use the result of this calculation as the financial impact to apply to your forecast. For example, if an earthquake has a 10% chance of occurring, but it would be a $10M impact to your organization, you may choose to enter this into your worst-case scenario as a $1M event. This creates balance across your risks as it is unlikely all would occur simultaneously.

Alternatively, you can create multiple business cases to capture and organize these events. As an example, you might choose to build five business cases:

- **Best Case**—upside events with a >25% probability of occurring.
- **Better Case**—upside events with a >50% probability of occurring.
- **Most-Likely**
- **Worse Case**—downside events with a >50% probability of occurring.
- **Worst Case**—downside events with a >25% probability of occurring.

You would put your earthquake in the worst-case business scenario at its full $10M financial impact.

Follow this process to incorporate business risks into your planning process:

1. Brainstorm material risks and opportunities.
2. Determine the likelihood and impact of each risk and opportunity.
3. For items that are negative in impact, adjust your "worse" and "worst" business cases:

    a) Activate, pause, or slow specific business initiatives.

    b) Adjust business activity levels such as Quantities, Shipments, or Hours.

4. Repeat the previous process for your positive items, but update your "better" and "best" business cases.

5. Regularly review the list of identified risks and opportunities and determine:

   a. Is the list still accurate? Do items need to be added, removed, or recategorized to another business case? (e.g., from "worse" to "worst")

   b. Are any of these risks or opportunities being realized? Is it time to activate contingency plans?

NO SURPRISES

Principle #5: *Assess Multiple Scenarios and Outcomes* is a critical element of Agile Planning to identify and plan emerging risks and opportunities. Principle #5 avoids surprises.

Doing this is not hard. You can embed multiple scenario analysis as a routine part of your process by using the other Principles—capturing and tagging initiatives to business scenarios, estimating your upside/downside business volumes, and documenting the business assumptions in your core forecast.

MAKE
PLANS
EASY TO
UPDATE

PRINCIPLE #6:
MAKE PLANS
EASY TO UPDATE

Organizations spend millions of dollars building new forecasting processes. After making this investment, many organizations end up with planners returning to spreadsheets within a few years.

If you design a cumbersome and time-consuming process, this could happen to you, and your forecasting process will fail. You need to set yourself up for success by making planning easy for your participants.

Principle #6: *Make Plans Easy to Update* helps forecasting succeed by getting your stakeholders to adopt the process.

HOW ORGANIZATIONS MAKE IT TOO HARD

Many forecasting processes are cumbersome, complex, and time-consuming for the organization. If you are sponsoring a rethink of your forecasting processes, you need to put your stakeholders first. You need to ensure that they will realize benefits greater than the time it takes them to keep their forecasts up to date.

One reason forecasting can be difficult occurs if you ask your operational teams like Manufacturing, Sales, Facilities, IT, and others to develop their Revenue and Cost forecasts using Finance's language. Finance will ask them to produce a forecast in terms of accounts, cost centers, legal entities, or currencies, for example. It is better to ask these areas to forecast in their language, not Finance's.

Operational teams should be forecasting in their own language using terms like labor hours, units, and material costs. You do not want to ask an operational team to develop a forecast in another language. When this happens, you are asking them to develop their own forecasting process that is separate from Finance's and subsequently convert to Finance's perspective. This creates low-value work for them.

You need to prioritize your stakeholders. Build a forecasting process that helps them first. Finance can get its financial data second.

Another practice that makes forecasting difficult is asking your participants to seek out and upload data into a planning tool. Operational teams are often asked to upload data from their operational systems, data like recent orders, invoices, business volumes, cost rates, or headcount. Do not add the burden of uploading data as a prerequisite to make a forecast update. Your participants do not have time to take on this work. You need to build operational data pipelines that automatically flow into the forecast. We will delve deeper into this when we get to Principle #8: *Detail Does Not Equal Accuracy.*

A third factor that makes forecasting difficult is the length of time it takes for participants to see updated information. At many organizations, it can take hours or days from the time someone makes a change to their forecast, and they can see a consolidated result. This is a bad experience; your process needs to update instantly.

If there is too much friction with the process, your stakeholders will avoid the process. Make it easy.

PLAN BY EXCEPTION

One foundational strategy to *Make Plans Easy to Update* is focusing a stakeholders' attention only when things go awry. This is called "planning by exception." Planning by exception dramatically reduces your stakeholders' forecasting workload and simultaneously increases the value they get from the process.

With today's modern tools, you can automatically text, email, or otherwise notify your stakeholders when a real-time trend moves away from their forecasted expectations. If their forecast remains on track, there is nothing for them to do, and they do not receive alerts.

Your stakeholders can set up automated forecasting rules for their area. They can choose assumptions to drive their forecast, like a trend or a business volume. Each time new actual results arrive, the forecasting tool automatically reforecasts using each stakeholder's chosen rules.

If the system detects a variance comparing the latest actuals versus their latest forecast, a stakeholder receives an automated alert to review the relevant part of their forecast. They might get an alert that a sales target, production volume, cost rate, or another measure is trending outside an acceptable range. If this happens, the stakeholder receives the alert, enters the system, reviews the alert, and decides on a course of action.

Building these feedback loops reduces the time and energy it takes the organization to forecast. It provides users with a real-time indication that something is wrong. It gets them in and out of the process quickly. It helps Finance because it ensures your stakeholders are frequently reviewing and updating their forecasts.

With the greater availability of data in the organization, these feedback loops can be made more real-time and frequent than traditional financial forecasting. A monthly or quarterly forecast can move to a more frequent update schedule: daily or weekly. The system automatically reforecasts using the latest information and monitors for new trends. A planner only needs to act if they receive an alert.

A few examples of how this concept can be applied to generate exception-based real-time alerts when the following events occur:

Manufacturing	<ul><li>Quantity produced yesterday is different than expected.</li><li>Most recent raw material purchases deviated from the expected price.</li><li>Labor hours are trending higher/lower than expected.</li><li>Machine hours are higher/lower than forecasted.</li></ul>

Sales	• Bookings were up last week.
	• New orders came in better than expected.
	• Average deal size is off from expected.
	• Mix between new/old clients is not as expected.
Services	• Hours billed are lower than expected.
	• Labor costs are up vs. expected.
	• Actual work completed is less than expected.
Staffing/HR	• Employee attrition is up vs. expected.
	• New hire starts vs. expected.
	• More open positions than planned.

When new operational data is loaded and compared to a forecast, and if an alert is generated, the owner gets a menu of options that can be used to resolve the issue, for example:

1. **Pushing a variance into the future**—This will keep their forecast as it was, and they will need to catch up in the coming days, weeks, and months. The business leader will need to make operational changes in their area to achieve their forecast.

2. **Dealing with the variance now**—by updating their forecast to align with the most recent results. This will incorporate the actual trend into the forecast. From a business perspective, they are accepting that the current trend is the reality on the ground.

Building interactive, early-warning feedback loops and getting your stakeholders planning by exception greatly reduces their workload. It keeps their forecasts up to date while helping them operationally manage their areas.

PLAN AT THE RIGHT LEVEL OF DETAIL

Principle #8: *Detail Does Not Equal Accuracy* goes into this in more depth, but another critical piece of keeping a forecast easy is to limit the amount of information a stakeholder needs to deal with. In simple terms, the right quantity of information is the least volume that allows managing their function while maintaining the velocity of the forecasting process.

If too much information is presented, it will become a difficult chore to download, analyze, and act on it. You need to strike a balance, presenting the right level of information so your stakeholders can quickly revise a forecast but detailed enough to be actionable.

The only way to do this is with a modern, cloud-based forecasting tool that combines operational and financial data and presents it in easily consumable alerts, notifications, and visualizations.

USE MODERN TOOLS

Today's modern, cloud-based planning and forecasting tools are easy to use and have matured from their older, on-premises cousins. These newer tools are accessible from anywhere over the internet, on the road, or in the office. They have modern user interfaces that make it obvious how to interact with them and require minimal training. These tools also allow users to collaborate and chat. Some work with voice assistants like Amazon Alexa, and you can ask them how your business is performing.

As forecasting tools have moved to the cloud, many of the blockers to getting a great forecasting process up and running are gone.

Planning tools used to be costly to purchase and maintain. You would purchase software from a vendor, buy servers, hire administrators, and periodically deal with software upgrades. Now, these tools are available as a monthly subscription. You sign up, receive your welcome email, and start building your agile forecasting process.

Older tools looked like spreadsheets but with less functionality. Since they looked like spreadsheets, Finance users understood them, but they were not a great fit for non-Finance users in Manufacturing, HR, Marketing, or out in the field.

Previously, planning and forecasting tools were constrained by small amounts of departmental data. This new generation of cloud-based planning tools can handle large operational datasets as well as your traditional financial information.

Another advantage of this new generation of tools is their ability to consolidate a planner's input without a long update cycle. As you make a change, you can see the change aggregate and propagate across the organization in real-time. This increases the dynamic nature of your forecasting process and eliminates another bottleneck to user adoption. This is a critical feature if you have a workforce spread across the world as there is no good time to take the tool down for "nightly" processing. The older generation of tools would require long processing cycles to aggregate forecast inputs into financial projections.

These cloud-based tools are accessible anywhere via web browsers and can be used on a computer, tablet, or phone. It is easy to get your users connected from home, the office, or out in the field. And, for Finance power-users, these products have plug-ins that can be used with Microsoft Office or Google Docs to allow more complicated modeling and reporting to occur directly within the world they know—spreadsheets.

You can set up easy-to-use, tablet-like navigations tailored to your non-Finance operational users. Easily understood user interfaces help users be productive without extensive training. When your users do need assistance, many of the tools allow you to post short videos a user can watch to get guidance when they need it.

Your users are not going to complain that the system is down or running slowly. The newest tools self-monitor their performance. If there is a problem, the vendor responds automatically.

The latest generation of tools remedies many of the issues that left a bad taste with users in the past. They just work and are easy to use.

The change from buying software to moving to a subscription reduces your organization's upfront cost, changes a capital investment to an operating expense, and gets you out of the cycle of installing, maintaining, and dealing with upgrades every few years. You get predictable pricing; most subscriptions invoice monthly based upon a per-user fee.

With subscription software, the burden shifts to the vendor to make sure you are getting value greater than the cost of your subscription. If you are not happy, they know you will cancel your subscription and switch to a different vendor. The onus is on the vendor to ensure you get a great experience.

Because vendors are competing for your business, they are cramming in as many features as they can. Most no longer require you to purchase individual features and are providing everything bundled in a single fee. Many vendors include core planning, financial reporting, long-range and strategic modeling, corporate consolidations, and account reconciliations as part of their fee (This varies by vendor).

These modern planning tools make it easier for you to adopt Principle #6: *Make Plans Easy to Update.*

THE GOLDEN AGE OF PLANNING TOOLS!

This is the golden age for cloud-based subscription planning and forecasting tools. If you are using spreadsheets or running an old planning tool, this is a good time to evaluate your options. There are more than 15 vendors in the *2019 Gartner Assessment of Enterprise Planning Tools*, and these vendors are fighting for your business.

If you start shopping for a tool, be sure to engage with multiple vendors, compare features, and make them fight for your business. To adopt Principle #6, here are some of the market leaders that you may want to consider to make planning easy:

- **Anaplan** (www.anaplan.com)—One of the few remaining independent planning vendors, traded on the New York Stock Exchange, and based in San Francisco. Anaplan is a modern cloud product that is gaining market share.
- **Workday Adaptive Insights** (www.adaptiveplanning.com)—Adaptive is steadily moving up in the market, competing successfully against established competitors like Oracle. Adaptive Insights is a newer product that Workday acquired in 2018.
- **OneStream XF** (www.onestreamsoftware.com)— OneStream is an up-and-comer that is gaining market position. They remain an independent organization, and their portfolio of forecasting capabilities is expanding.
- **Oracle EPM Planning** (www.oracle.com/epm)— Oracle rebuilt their planning applications for the cloud. They are the market leader according to Gartner's 2019 ranking. Their pricing is competitive with other players in the market, and Oracle EPM Planning has a rich set of features.

GET AN EXPERT'S HELP

Once you have chosen your cloud software tool, you need to find an expert to bridge the gap between your business and your chosen software.

You need a partner that understands your business industry, revenue model, and size. You need an implementor that can provide forecasting expertise and leading practices. You want their help to build a solid and flexible foundation that can change and grow with your organization over time.

Be wary of consulting companies that only provide technical expertise. Building a new forecasting project is not an IT project. It is a business process project. Ensure your consultants are experts in forecasting best practices and can bring those processes to life in your chosen technology.

A good consulting partner will help you succeed as you adopt an agile, dynamic forecasting process.

As you evaluate different consulting partners, ask them:

- Can they provide expertise for different parts of the project—business process, industry, and technical expertise?
- Do they have expertise in your type of organization? Do they understand your organization's inputs, processes, and outputs? You do not want to teach your consultants how your business works.
- Can they provide project accelerators based on similar projects? The best consulting companies have prebuilt quick-starts that can quickly get you using your cloud planning tool, get value, and then build upon that foundation.
- Do they have the right people and expertise to help drive the organizational change to ensure people adopt a new forecasting process? You will need help with the people side of deploying a new forecasting process: communicating how processes are changing, making sure people feel confident living in the new process with training, job aids, help desks, and even migrating old spreadsheets to the new process.

Once you start living in your process, the process needs to evolve. Principle #9: *The World Keeps Changing— Change With It!* reminds you that your organization, customers, and operating environment are continuously evolving. Your consulting expert needs to walk with you as you adopt a new forecasting process. You will need their expertise to make sure that you incorporate feedback from your stakeholders and evolve the process over time. Your consulting partner can help you implement continuous feedback cycles using focus groups, surveys, and one-on-one interviews with stakeholders.

As new features are added to your cloud subscription, you will need their guidance to get the most from the software tools as they evolve.

Good consulting companies can augment your team with on-demand support to avoid adding staff for routine maintenance, such as updating your organizational structure or getting ready for a new budget cycle.

The best consulting companies work hard to develop behind-the-scenes relationships with software vendors, and they cultivate contacts that range from software developers to Executives. These contacts come in handy when you face an issue with the software and need help!

Like any buying decision, shop and find the right partner to help you create Agile Planning in your organization. Make sure they have business expertise for your type of organization and industry. Make sure they are experts with the vendor's software. Make sure they understand that this is a business process project and not a technology project.

Check references and interview consultants before you make a final decision!

YOU ONLY GET ONE CHANCE

You only get one chance to build agile, modern, and effective planning in your organization. You need to use the right software and find the right experts to position you for success.

Use techniques like "planning by exception" to escalate alerts when trends start to diverge from reality. Build automated data pipelines to operational data, so your participants do not need to load data before updating their forecasts. Make the process as real-time as possible while making it operationally valuable, so planners update and act upon their forecast every day.

Any friction that makes it hard for your stakeholders to adopt the process increases your project's risk of failure. You need to make it easy.

MANY SMALL PLANS ARE BETTER THAN 1 BIG PLAN

PRINCIPLE #7: MANY SMALL PLANS ARE BETTER THAN ONE BIG PLAN

In a perfect world, every stakeholder will have their plan linked with all the other plans in the organization. When one area of the organization updates their forecast and impacts someone else, downstream teams will see the demand or supply of resources change in their forecasts. If Sales sells more units, Operations needs to ramp up production, Purchasing needs to buy more, and HR needs to start recruiting.

Most organizations sponsor a single, monolithic plan managed by Finance. Different parts of the organization contribute to the central plan, but each team does it differently, building their own processes and buying their own forecasting tools. These teams develop their own planning processes that are disconnected from each other. Each area needs to coordinate through emails and meetings to reflect their interdependencies with each other's forecasts. This leads to delays, errors, and miscommunication.

Breaking the forecasting process into smaller, interconnected components makes the forecast process faster and easier. Build a process that works for each area in the language of their function. Each function should plan at a level of detail that makes sense for them using their key elements such as customers, items, projects, products, locations, channels, machines, or employees. The process handles the burden of converting each area's operational plan into Finance's perspective.

As you create Agile Planning in your organization, Principle #7: *Many Small Plans are Better than One Big Plan* ensures that you provide each function with a forecasting process that makes sense for them.

HOW DOES AN ORGANIZATION FAIL?

#1 It Grows Over Time until it Collapses!

As you create more dependencies within any single area of your planning process, it will become bloated and slow. Often, you will see this happen when an organization has a single forecasting database that tries to accommodate everybody's needs.

An example of this is attempting to help the Sales team develop commission plans in the same system IT uses to forecast their projects. These two processes are distinct and unrelated and should not co-exist within the same spreadsheet or system.

This happens when an organization cannot or does not want to create focused solutions for each area. This is a band-aid approach to provide quick fixes. When I see quick fixes like this, I know that a slow and complex forecasting process is not far behind.

Another problem occurs when an organization uses an old planning software package that was implemented many years ago. A single old, creaky application that tries to handle all aspects of the planning process. This is akin to everyone in the organization attempting to forecast in a single spreadsheet at the same time. Every input, calculation, update, and report funnels through a single choke point.

As the number of participants from different business functions increases, completing the planning process becomes a dance. Finance micro-manages the forecast timeline to get it completed on time. Participants are frustrated by tight deadlines and long wait times to see results. Participants work nights and weekends to find a window to make their updates to meet deadlines.

A better approach is to isolate each forecasting process into discrete, stand-alone components to increase velocity allowing stakeholders to focus only on their areas without having to coordinate with other teams to meet tight deadlines.

#2 Trying to Make Everyone Happy!

It is a once-in-a-decade opportunity when an organization builds a new planning process. The organization gets excited!

Other teams with their own planning and forecasting issues ask to have their requirements addressed. Program sponsors attempt to keep other leaders happy and agree to take on more project requirements.

Instead of applying Principle #7 and creating focused, interconnected solutions for these additional needs, they attempt to solve them within the same project phase and budget. This leads to compromises by attempting to solve too many requirements at once.

#3 One Mega-Planning Application to Rule Them All!

As the organization tries to solve everyone's needs at once, you might end up with a single, convoluted planning and forecasting application... like you were trying to replace in example #1.

Most cloud-based planning applications work most efficiently when they are constructed of many focused forecasting models. Small and nimble planning models developed for each area of your organization will be faster and easier to maintain, and they will meet each area's specific needs.

If you see a project team trying to create a single mega-planning application to solve everyone's needs, it will not work. It will be slow and suffer from long cycles to update data. It will be complicated to understand. It will be difficult to evolve when the organization changes.

MAKE LOTS OF PLANS

If monolithic and cumbersome forecasting processes do not work, the alternative is to build smaller, more focused forecasting processes. These smaller processes must interconnect to facilitate collaboration among teams.

Start by inventorying all of the different business functions in your organization. Each function will likely need a unique forecasting process—for example, Manufacturing, Operations, Sales, HR, Legal, Marketing, Purchasing, Facilities, and IT. Your business units that have differing business models will need separate revenue forecasting models.

When different businesses and functions share similar business models, they can share a standard forecasting capability. You do not need to build redundant forecasting solutions. For example, your short-cycle manufacturers can share a single revenue forecasting capability. Your project-based service functions can share a project forecasting capability. If you have multiple Sales teams across the organization, they can share a common commission forecasting application. Defining security roles can limit access to individual teams within these shared capabilities.

Next, you need to map out the interdependencies between different teams and functions across the organization. You need to identify the interconnections between each area's forecasts so that when one area demands resources, the supply side can see and react to the need. Learn from each area how they communicate their supply of resources to match the demand for resources from other functions. Seek to understand how managing their supply and demand translates into a financial revenue and cost forecast.

You need to ensure everyone shares a common language of forecasting to facilitate the fast consolidation of sub-plans. A shared taxonomy like this avoids using spreadsheets to translate sub-plans into a centralized forecast. Your sub-processes will unfold at a deeper level of detail—like marketing campaigns, clients, and products—but these elements need to correlate to the organization's financial Chart of Accounts.

A shared definition of common organizational structures, such as legal entities and departments, will ensure that each area's forecasts can consolidate without human intervention.

As you develop deeper sub-planning processes to accommodate each function's unique needs, you will notice the granularity increasing. Each area will want to focus on more detailed modeling for their area for things like product lines, inventory items, customers, projects, campaigns, leads, prospects, people, and so on. Still, this increasing granularity will always consolidate to an enterprise-wide view.

You can visualize this increasing level of detail through this ***pyramid of planning granularity***. The top of the pyramid manages the summarized, Executive-level information. The middle of the pyramid contains shared planning capabilities that can be used across the organization. The bottom of the pyramid manages operational forecasting aligned to individual business units and functional areas.

By deepening the granularity of modular planning across the organization, aligned to each area's needs, the organization and the forecasting process gain several benefits, such as the ability to:

1. Adjust, replace, or alter the planning process for a single part of the business without impacting everyone.
2. Accommodate changes to business structures or business models—if the organization acquires a new business or product, a portion of the planning process can be quickly adjusted.

3. Reorganize parts of the business or combine parts of the business as the organization evolves. The financial process and systems environment will not be the hold-up accommodating internal reorganizations.

The top of the pyramid represents the consolidated, Executive-level, financial-centric view driven by Finance, including:

- Consolidated P&L, Balance Sheet, and Cash Flow reporting
- Management P&Ls for the organization—with corporate & shared costs allocated to business units.

The middle of the pyramid offers capabilities that are shared across the organization, such as:

- Expense planning
- Headcount planning
- Initiative and capital investment planning

The bottom of the pyramid represents the business unit and functional sub-forecasting processes, tailored to each area's specific needs. These capabilities help forecast, manage, and run parts of the organization, including:

- Revenue (Sales) planning
- Manufacturing planning
- Raw materials planning
- IT project planning
- Marketing campaign planning
- Legal cost planning
- Tax planning
- Sales quota and commission planning

If your organization can break the forecasting process into smaller, modular processes, the overall process becomes more adaptable, flexible, and nimble.

MODULAR PLANNING

By breaking your planning process into smaller, more manageable modular processes, you can realize several benefits versus building a large, monolithic solution:

1. You build stakeholder-first forecasting tailored to their needs, not Finance's. This stakeholder-first approach provides them with a forecast capability that helps them run their businesses. The overall organization benefits by having a quality forecast created by the people running each part of the organization.
2. Planning unfolds in the stakeholder's language—customers, products, etc.—and will make sense to them. It will require less training and have less friction when driving adoption.
3. Smaller processes allow business users more opportunity to control the process—forecasting more or less frequently than the corporate mother ship—at the right frequency for running their businesses.
4. This approach improves stakeholders' user experience and work/life balance. Smaller, more nimble, focused processes perform better and have fewer dependencies.
5. "Rome wasn't built in a day." A modular approach allows you to phase in capabilities over time.

CONNECT YOUR PLANS

Once you have your sub-forecasts, they need to interconnect. When one part of the organization updates their forecast, dependent teams should feel the impacts in their forecasts.

There are two fundamental types of connections to think about when designing a planning process:

- Summary to Detail
- Supply and Demand

#1 Summary to Detail

Traversing the pyramid from top to bottom ensures that plans can be shared, exchanged, and consolidated across the organization. The pyramid's foundation is a standardized nomenclature called a "planning chart of accounts." A common planning chart of accounts allows everyone to speak the same language, from the most detailed operational planning process to the corporate summary view. A planning chart of accounts provides shared definitions of accounts, legal entities, business units, and products.

Where it makes sense, operational and functional areas can expand to a deeper level of granularity than the common chart provides so they can appropriately model their businesses. If a business expands to a level deeper than the shared definition, they need to map their additional detail to the shared definition. This flexibility ensures that everyone's forecasts can consolidate cleanly while facilitating other business unit-specific details.

As an example, in a company with two separate businesses—one with a product-based revenue model and one with a services-based revenue model—both share a common definition of a **Business Unit** and **Line of Business**. However, each business defined an additional level of detail to support forecasting their distinct revenue models.

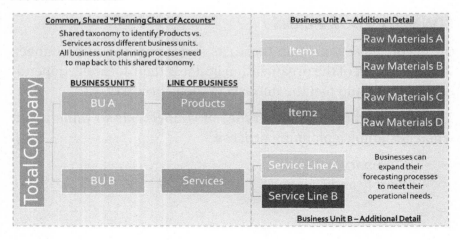

In this example, Business Unit A plans by Items and Materials, whereas Business Unit B plans by Service Line. Each has a separate forecasting process where they use these additional details.

To facilitate the overall consolidation of results, both businesses ensure their Items and Service Lines map to the shared definition of Business Unit and Line of Business.

This shared nomenclature, process, and tools have the added benefit of making your organization a better place to work. Employees have more freedom to transfer between different functions and business units, as they do not need to relearn the language and mechanics of forecasting. They can focus on learning the new parts of their jobs.

#2 Supply and Demand

The other aspect of linking modular plans together is to connect the demand for resources in one area with an increase in supply in another. As one part of the business experiences a change in activity, it will impact another in terms of hiring, purchasing raw materials, internal projects, providing working capital, and so on.

Modeling these relationships between functions will streamline the communication of supply and demand across the organization. As the integration between different processes increases, the organization can communicate and react faster. The latest cloud-based planning platforms provide features to create linkages between areas.

These interconnections need a few guardrails to prevent forecasting chaos. As one area presents a change to another, the receiving area needs to accept or reject that proposal. Changes should not propagate from one function to another without a form of approval on the receiving side. This avoids one area making an error and having that error spread throughout the forecasting process.

To make these systematic linkages work, you need to support collaboration by doing the following:

1. Provide social features and messaging within the planning platform. Planners in different areas need to chat, comment, and annotate within the forecast.

2. Create working sandboxes for each area so planners can work on their part of the plan in private. When their part of the forecast is ready, they can publish from their sandbox to a shared view. This ensures that each small change does not propagate and impact another forecast until the sender is ready to publish.

3. Once a team pushes their needs to someone else's forecast, the recipient should receive an alert that there is a pending forecast adjustment. The impacted team can accept, adjust, or collaborate.

4. Finally, the system needs to provide robust change auditing and logging. This way, everyone involved can see who made a change, why they made the change, and the original and revised values. In a modern, fast-moving organization, your stakeholders need to be able to answer their own questions about who made a change and why.

MANY SMALL PLANS ARE BETTER THAN ONE BIG PLAN

Principle #7: *Many Small Plans are Better than One Big Plan* breaks large, monolithic planning processes into smaller, stand-alone processes that focus on specific parts of the organization. These smaller plans are at a level of detail that provides operational information to help run their businesses—elements like products, items, SKUs, projects, people, or clients.

These elements align to a common taxonomy that facilitates consolidation up the pyramid and exchanging supply & demand requests across the pyramid. This shared taxonomy benefits your employees as they have more flexibility to move around without the associated learning curve of learning a new forecasting language.

Link multiple planning processes together to increase forecasting velocity. Facilitate the exchange of requests to supply or demand labor, resources, and funds across the organization. Cloud-based planning tools can automate these requests between teams by allowing them to accept, revise, and iterate with each other.

PRINCIPLE #8:
DETAIL DOES NOT
EQUAL ACCURACY

Many organizations assume that if they use as much detailed data as possible, their forecasts will be more accurate.

Principle #8: *Detail Does Not Equal Accuracy* finds the right balance between limiting the amount of information a planner needs to assess when updating a forecast but still providing enough detail so you can manage your organization.

Too often, organizations plan the minutiae, asking their planners to process data first, and forecast second. If your forecast is too detailed, you consume your limited forecasting resources reviewing data versus thinking about the organization's future. Asking a planner to work with too much detail causes resistance to the process. This friction violates Principle #6: *Make Plans Easy to Update.*

You can achieve a forecast informed by real-time operational without burdening planners. You can do this by building data pipelines that acquire front-line data, inform the forecasting process on an increasingly frequent basis, and keep the planner focused on forecasting.

IOT CHANGES EVERYTHING

Many Finance teams have not taken advantage of the new, real-time data sources that are available within their organizations. The Internet of Things (IoT) is permeating every industry, organization, and business, including yours. This term refers to the collection of data from every device and process.

As your customers and employees interact with the organization, every interaction is recorded. Your forecasting processes can use this telemetry from your prospects, customers, employees, machines, and processes to provide insight into the latest business trends.

As the availability of this information increases, you can integrate it into your forecasting to build a business early-warning system. This early-warning system compares expected forecasts against real-time activity. If real-time activity begins trending differently than expected, a stakeholder receives an alert to take action.

This is the opposite of the old way, waiting a few weeks after month-end to see financial results and then realizing you missed your budget.

As customers and employees interact with your organization, these interactions are recorded real-time. Signals are collected from prospects as they hit your sales and marketing assets, like websites or call centers, and from customers as they consume your organization's products and services. Signals are also collected from your employees as they interact with the organization's processes—from how fast they respond, their efficiency, effectiveness, and so on.

You can use this extremely detailed information to run your organization and support forecasting.

The trick is using this information without violating the Nine Principles. This operational, real-time data needs to be presented in an easy-to-consume, useful way without being overwhelming.

HOW DO COMPANIES FAIL?

Most companies have not integrated their real-time business signals into their forecasting process. In today's world, most planners work with two styles of forecast information:

1. Highly aggregated financial information from their organization's general ledger system. This information is at the end of the data pipeline, comes from a financial

perspective, is weeks old, and is not directly tied to the operational business levers that produced the financial results.

2. Think of an organization's management P&L, with Revenues (Sales) and Cost-of-Sales, but with little insight into production volumes, raw material costs, or customer behavior.
3. Extremely detailed operational information, representing every possible item in the business master files.
4. Imagine planning by every single product, client, or employee record.

#1 Too Summarized and Disconnected

In many organizations, forecasting is centralized with Finance, and operational teams do not actively participate in the process. Finance develops the organization's forecast for the whole organization. At the end of the forecast, each area receives their budget targets.

When organizations take this centralized, Finance-centric forecasting approach, Finance generally starts with the end in mind: the financial statements. Finance forecasts each P&L line—Revenues (Sales), Returns, Allowances, Cost-of-Goods Sold—using trends and a few simple business levers like Quantity and Average Selling Price.

As individual functions need more detail to manage their organizations, they begin modeling at a deeper level of detail using their own operational data. Each area builds their own operational forecasting models disconnected from the broader Finance view.

#2 Too Detailed—Counting Beans

As your operational teams push for more accuracy and more actionable information to run their businesses, they gravitate toward using the raw operational data they have at their fingertips.

This begins the voyage to increasing forecasting work by building large spreadsheets. These spreadsheets will be hundreds of thousands of rows long, planning the future activity levels for every item in their areas. Planners will go to their ordering or production systems, download everything they can into a spreadsheet, and review it all line-by-line. For each row of data, they guess what they think will happen in the future.

People feel good about planning at this level. It takes a lot of time and effort—but does not necessarily create a better forecast.

If you see people in your organization downloading the following types of information into a spreadsheet to update a forecast, be warned:

- Every customer's order
- Every employee's pay rate
- Every accounts payable invoice
- Every employee's timesheet
- Every asset, customer, vendor, or similar register

If your organization is small, this works when you have a few thousand items. However, you cannot scale from thousands to millions of data elements. People will buy time shifting these hyper-detailed spreadsheets into a planning tool. Taking a flawed process and putting it into another tool will not fix the inefficiency caused by using a hyper-detailed forecasting methodology.

This is the ***paradox of planning***: the more detailed the process gets, the less valuable it is; it takes longer to update, it is difficult to change, and it is hard to see the big picture. In short, it can be hard to see the forest for the trees.

As we covered in Principle #6: *Make Plans Easy to Update*, the latest cloud tools provide [essentially] infinite capacity and scalability. Forecast sponsors are exacerbating their forecasting inefficiencies with these new tools by making larger datasets available to their planners. Planners spend their days collecting and processing data—primarily busy work. Many organizations will add staff to keep up as the data volume grows. This is not a winning strategy.

In Principle #1, we discussed the example of a large US company conducting a hyper-detailed labor expense forecasting process for their 50,000-employee workforce. In theory, this process should have generated an accurate labor expense forecast. After all, every month, 200 financial analysts reviewed every employee's HR record. They reviewed HR's data for accuracy and layered on expected compensation changes, transfers, and terminations.

In reality, their financial analysts had limited time each month to complete the process. Since they were under a deadline, they had to move fast and rush through the process—they skimmed through the detail and fixed any obvious errors and variances. Did employees transfer or terminate unexpectedly? Were there compensation changes? Were there any new, unplanned hires?

Their forecasting process repeated month after month. A new HR roster would update in their planning tool, and their financial analysts would sort through and reconcile their 50,000 employees over and over.

The process failed after a few years.

Management attempted to make the process less burdensome by changing the cadence from monthly to quarterly. Finally, several business units abandoned this process because it consumed more time than it created in value. Those businesses found other ways to forecast labor costs.

Another example: a property and casualty insurance company would forecast each of their 20,000 insurance policies four times a year.

Their team would download each client's policy information from their billing system into a spreadsheet. They would go line by line, deciding whether each policy would renew, grow, or leave. This took weeks!

For the most part, they assumed clients would just renew.

In both the labor planning and insurance planning examples, both organizations had a perceived feeling of security from analyzing all of the detail. In the end, these approaches consumed resources, adding up to thousands of hours of effort with little value to show.

No one can forecast the future perfectly. Attempting to predict the future by asking your team to analyze every element of your business ends in guessing. There will be attrition, changes, and events you cannot expect. It is impossible to know which clients will leave, go out of business, or just change.

As Principle #1 states, *Focus on the Important Things*.

Getting more operational data to inform your planning process is a goal supported by the Principles. Still, you need to use this operational data in the right way by combining it with automation. Without automation, the **paradox of planning** will continue to make the planning process slower and less effective as the volume of data increases.

GOLDILOCKS: NOT TOO HOT OR COLD

As your business grows, you will reach a point where a people-driven, hyper-detailed forecasting process cannot keep up. You need to create a forward-thinking process, automated, and informed by data, yet still manageable, easy-to-use, and trusted by the people who need to rely on it to develop operationally relevant guidance.

To do this, you can adopt several strategies to find the right level of detail to provide accuracy but remaining fast and nimble:

1. Follow the 80/20 Rule (Principle #1: *Focus on the Important Things*).
2. Map business signals to business levers (Principle #3: *Derive Financial Forecasts from Real-World Plans*).
3. Use automation to monitor business signals and do the bulk of the forecasting grunt work.

80/20 Rule

Agile Principle #1: *Focus on the Important Things* focuses on the important 20% that drives your business while minimizing the effort put into forecasting the routine 80%. This is the #1 strategy to ensure that you plan at the right level of detail to run your business.

In simple terms, do not plan every single customer or product. Take the top 20% of your population, then use simpler, automated strategies for the remaining lower-impact items.

At the insurance client that was forecasting 20,000 policies, they asked themselves: How can we increase accuracy and speed at the same time? They decided to change the process. Instead of forecasting all of their 20,000 policies, they realized that 80% of their policy revenue came from 100 customers. They focused their efforts on the 100 customers that really mattered.

This limited the scope to a manageable effort and brought the discussion to a higher maturity level. Instead of forecasting revenue one-by-one in a spreadsheet, the team discussed how they could grow those 100 customer relationships. They used the decisions they made during those conversations to inform their forecast changes.

For the routine long tail of their policy portfolio, they followed Principle #3 using automated trending to revise their forecast. Their policy-writing system now calculates the policy count and an average premium-per-policy for this part of the portfolio. This information is automatically loaded into the forecasting tool, and the system revises the forecast.

Map Business Signals to Business Levers

In the coming years, you may want to dip your toes into using your in-house IoT data to inform your forecasts. Do this carefully, taking great care not to overwhelm your planners. They should never see the underlying detail, but the data should be frequently updated and timely. This is the practical application of linking your real-time data to the business volume levers we discussed in Principle #3: *Derive Financial Forecasts from Real-World Plans*.

In a computer-hosting company, like the cloud software vendors that provide forecasting tools, these IoT signals are logs. These logs record metrics like the number of logins, storage consumption, response times, customer service tickets, help desk minutes, and the amount of electricity used. This data is collected by the second and can form billions of log entries.

You cannot provide raw data like this in its granular form.

To do this, you need to aggregate raw IoT log data into volume measures useful for forecasting. An example is to aggregate this information to a business activity level volume such as "storage consumed." Your storage consumption trend is a business lever that drives your revenues, expenses, and additional investments.

IOT measures like this need to be aggregated and transmitted to the forecasting process in a cleansed form on a daily, weekly, or monthly basis. A data point like "storage consumed" will be comprised of billions of rows of log data collected across many servers and clients.

A business signal like this is easily applied to financial forecasting and provides the groundwork to build an early-warning system for your organization. If a customer starts using more or less of a service than expected, you can get an alert to take action as described in Principle #6: *Make Plans Easy to Update*. If a customer stays on-trend, there is nothing to forecast.

A final note about adding more detail into your forecasting process: make sure you solve the right problem. In many cases, you do not need to add more detail.

In the HR example we discussed, as an alternative to forecasting the career aspirations of each of their 50,000 employees, they could have developed a less detailed and more elegant approach. Their process started with the employee roster, and they built a forecasting process involving 200 analysts around it. Alternatively, they could have taken a blank sheet of paper and found a more straightforward and faster approach.

When asked to add more detail, step back and ask if there is a faster, simpler, more elegant, and strategic approach.

Use Automation to Monitor Your Business Signals

As we discussed in Principle #6: *Make Plans Easy to Update*, planning by exception focuses your stakeholders' attention on where they need to take action when real-world trends start to change.

You can speed this feedback loop to be real-time if you can link your operational data with your forecasting process. As the real-world changes on a daily basis, you can inform the process of how things are going on an hourly or daily basis. This avoids the lag you get when you make the forecasting process solely dependent on financial data that is only available after the month is complete.

You should consider integrating some of your IoT operational data sources into your forecasting process to gain insight into the real-time health of your organization. This improves the ability of your operational managers to run their parts of the organization and react to changes before it is too late.

Modern big-data technologies available from Amazon, Microsoft, Oracle, and others can collect these real-time signals and continuously aggregate them into useful information.

A few things to remember about leveraging hyper-detailed IOT data and transforming it into usable forecasting business levers:

- Business signals are collected every second/minute and are collected across every single interaction with a device or service. This data is hyper-detailed and usually comes in the form of computer log files. It must be aggregated to be useful; studying a subset will not provide you with any knowledge of what is happening.
- Many of these measures need to be aggregated and compared across time to be useful. They might be stated in absolute terms like "count" or "total minutes," but they likely need to be derived into "% change" or "hours/minutes used over the past month." These types of business levers will let you see in real-time if your business is growing, stagnating, or slowing.

A vendor providing software subscriptions might monitor the storage consumed by clients on individual devices down to the second. This information might be used for technical reasons to operate infrastructure or to invoice clients.

To turn this information into a valuable lever for forecasting, you need to create a measure like "weekly storage consumed by client." This is a measure that can be used to watch the business. Behind the scenes, it is tied into real-world, operational-detailed logs.

This is nirvana—forecasting is out of the weeds—but it is driven by real-time real-world trends.

The newest cloud-based planning tools can take these business levers and monitor them against expectations. If the trend starts to shift, your stakeholders get an alert that "something is wrong!" They can review and assess if there is a material change happening in the business.

DETAIL DOES NOT EQUAL ACCURACY

Remember the **paradox of planning**: As you ask your stakeholders to plan in more detail, the less accurate and more time-consuming your forecast will be.

Many organizations have a false sense of security that forecasting with more granularity will create a more accurate forecast. Being too detailed gets your participants focused on data and not the more significant questions of where they are headed.

If you can aggregate and cleanse detailed data into usable business metrics, you can provide real-time insights at a consumable level of detail. Take advantage of the increasingly real-time signals coming in from your IoT-enabled organization and map these signals to useful business levers. Build automated data pipelines that constantly collect data and compare it to the expectations set during the forecasting process.

Never ask planners to forecast at an extreme level of detail!

You can utilize more data behind the scenes if you let the technology do the heavy lifting. But before you add more data to the process, make sure you solve the right problem. You might not need more data. You might need a better forecasting methodology.

PRINCIPLE #9:
THE WORLD KEEPS
CHANGING—
CHANGE WITH IT!

Your organization is in a state of constant evolution, and your forecasting process needs to keep up.

Products and services are discontinued. New ones are introduced. New revenue and business models no longer fit within existing methodologies. Business acquisitions and reorganizations change the type of information leaders need. Areas of the business mature and need more sophisticated forecasts.

Embrace the change. Continuously improve. Stay relevant.

Every forecasting process starts as a project with limited funding, resources, and time. These constraints lead to compromises, and even on Day-1 of your new process, there will be opportunities to improve. As people adopt the new process, they will identify enhancements to make it better.

Principle #9: *The World Keeps Changing—Change With It!* ensures that your forecasting process includes an innovation feedback loop to identify and incorporate ongoing enhancements.

HOW DO COMPANIES FAIL?

When I visit new clients, I often see an army of financial analysts updating spreadsheets. When I ask, "What are you doing?" the answer is usually, "Updating the monthly forecast."

The irony is that many of these spreadsheets were created years ago by people that are no longer there. Those financial analysts pull the levers on their forecasting machine without understanding why they do it. The forecast is on autopilot and runs itself every month. There is little innovation or introspection into the current process.

When I assess the maturity of forecasting, I ask the team:

How often do you run your forecast?

Too many organizations run annual or quarterly forecasting cycles; This is too slow.

In our current world, a new competitor can be created in weeks by tapping into private equity, cloud computing, and outsourced fulfillment. The barriers to entry for many businesses are low. By the time you see your quarterly results in your general ledger, 45 days after the period closes, you may already be under siege by a competitor or another macroeconomic trend.

Companies must adopt dynamic, continuous, operationally integrated planning that is constantly updated with real-time frontline data.

When was the last time you evaluated your forecast accuracy?

You should take a step back and determine whether the forecast is any good.

The best forecasting processes review how closely their forecasts predict the actual results. If the forecast lands far from the actuals, positively or negatively, they ask themselves how the process failed. They use these exceptions to improve the process, so the same issue does not occur next time.

The fixes can be big or small.

In some cases, a variance calls attention to an element changing its nature or materiality. As discussed in Principle #1: *Focus On The Important Things*, an item could shift from being fixed or variable in nature, or the element needs to move closer to the business owner as discussed in Principle #7: *Many Small Plans are Better than One Big Plan*.

Other times, the variance calls attention to simpler issues. You may have a planner that requires additional training. Or a participant requires additional time to complete their part of the forecasting process.

When did you last take a fresh look at the methodologies within the forecast process?

Most organizations are complacent with their forecasting. They keep going with the same process month after month. Every year or two, repeat the assessment in Principle #1 to determine if the organization's planning approach chosen for each item continues to make sense.

In parallel, continuously monitor the process for an increasing number of recurring variances. A growing number of variances over time could signal items are changing in their nature (e.g., from fixed to variable) or have outgrown their forecasting methodologies.

Have you reached out to other teams like Sales, Manufacturing, IT, HR, Legal, Marketing, and others to see how you can collaborate and link your forecasting processes together?

The best forecasters work with their internal partners to make sure that, when one area needs more resources, those impacts ripple to their supporting teams. Does your team's forecasting process integrate the upstream and downstream inputs into other forecasts? As an example, if the organization plans to increase Revenues (Sales) next year, is HR in the loop, so they know they need to ramp up hiring? Is Manufacturing in the loop, so they know they need to increase production?

Principle #7: *Many Small Plans are Better than One Big Plan* strives for integration among each other's plans while keeping it manageable with Principle #6: *Make Plans Easy to Update.*

Is anyone using the output of your efforts? Have you surveyed your internal customers and participants?

Periodically, ask your internal customers if the organization's published forecasts and budgets are helpful. Ask for specific examples of how they took the forecast and made a business decision. The answer to this question can be a great insight into providing more actionable information.

Meet with business leaders in the organization and ask them which forecast-related reports, analyses, schedules, and presentations they use. If you are using a reporting tool or document repository, most can provide a log of how often an item is accessed. You might be surprised how much work your team does that is not used.

Have you introduced new products or services over the past year? Did you update your forecasting process to accommodate these new offerings?

Natural and routine organizational changes should be integrated into the forecasting process. If you have introduced a new product or service, ask your team how this new product is reflected within the forecast. This new product or service introduction may be an opportunity to facilitate a discussion around evolving part of the forecasting process using the Nine Principles to include additional real-time data or to create a more front-line focused planning capability.

As new datasets become available, have you incorporated them into your process?

As we saw with Principle #8: *Detail Does Not Equal Accuracy*, a key change in the last few years has been the ability to collect business signals in real-time. This gives the organization an early-warning system to monitor real-world activity against your forecasts.

Periodically, ask your business teams if there are new data sources the forecast can tap into. Ask if there have been any new internal systems implemented in HR, IT, Facilities, Marketing, Legal, Manufacturing, and so on.

Ask your Product and Sales teams if they introduced any new products or services that collect real-time signals about customer activity; if so, these can be leveraged to inform the forecasting process.

Finally, does the forecast have any impact on business leaders' actions? Or, do they wait for actual results to make a decision?

If the forecast process is not helpful to your business leaders, it needs to evolve. Principle #9: *The Real World Keeps Changing—Change With It!* is a reminder to keep evolving, adapting the process over time. The Principles can create a forecast process that is dynamic, easy-to-use, and provides value for business leaders to run their organizations.

MONITOR AND IMPROVE THE PROCESS

Your forecasting process must evolve. Capture feedback, identify opportunities, and implement improvements.

Start by capturing feedback with surveys and focus groups. Ask your forecast participants to explain what is working in the process and what needs to be improved. You should rotate topics over time, focusing on gaining feedback in a limited number of forecasting areas at any one time.

To engineer a continuous improvement feedback loop, follow these steps:

1. Survey your participants and incorporate their feedback to make the process better. They are the ones executing the process and have the most to say.
2. Conduct after-forecast assessments to identify what worked well and what failed. Constantly strive to remove blockers that encumber your participants.
3. Ask users of forecast information how it helps them make business decisions. Ask for recent examples. If there are none, ask why.
4. Review the cause of recurring forecast variances. If they are process-related, fix the process.
5. Look for elements that have changed in their nature; e.g., a fixed item now moves with business activity levels.

6. If a part of the business has grown in complexity. The forecast may need to be subdivided into smaller focused processes, as discussed in Principle #7.
7. Continuously incorporate new products, data sources, and functions into the process
8. If using a modern system, review usage and utilization logs to ensure adoption is growing over time. Look for users that have stopped participating in the process.
9. Implement processes to measure the bottlenecks and efficiency of the process. Over time, you can measure the forecast accuracy, number of recurring variances, the reduction in the number of spreadsheets, the addition of any new spreadsheets, and the duration it takes for the organization to complete a forecast. This information, charted over time, will direct you to areas that require attention.

REASSESS YOUR PROCESS USING THE NINE PRINCIPLES

Time and change are working against you, reducing the value of the process. At least once a year, take a step back and think about the big picture, and determine how to fight back.

Periodically, review the health of your forecasting process and your adoption of the Nine Principles by asking:

- Are we focusing on the manageable?
- Are the right items planned using trend methodologies versus business volumes?
- Are we planning real-world initiatives?
- Are we deriving financial forecasts from real-world plans?
- Do our plans align with our long-term goals?
- Are we assessing multiple scenarios and outcomes?
- Is our plan easy to update?
- Do we have new customer-centric data that we can use to inform the forecasting process?
- Can we break our forecast into smaller sub-processes?

- Is the forecast close enough to the people running the organization?
- Are we planning with too much detail?
- Are we using automation as an early warning system to alert us when reality diverges from our plans?

THE WORLD KEEPS CHANGING—CHANGE WITH IT!

Principle #9: *The Real World Keeps Changing—Change With It!* encourages monitoring the process, gaining feedback, and driving improvement. First, keep up with organizational changes like new products, services, and data. Second, solicit continuous feedback from your participants and internal customers.

Stop the decay caused by organizational and external changes from eating away at your agile and nimble forecasting process.

Do not let the process stagnate!

NINE PRINCIPLES TO LIGHT YOUR WAY

When *The Nine Principles of Agile Planning* are in balance, they combine and reinforce each other creating incredible strength and durability. Use this strength to achieve nimble forecasting that guides your organization in a changing world.

You are likely already living some of the Nine Principles today. Build upon your strengths and create new capabilities where you are weak. If you can do both, you will have a modern, connected, agile, and nimble forecasting process that stays relevant over time.

When the time comes to invest in a new forecasting process, it will take money, people, and time, with a significant opportunity cost of not working on other things. This investment is no different from developing a new product, building a factory, or hiring staff. Any business investment like this must earn an ROI.

The Nine Principles achieve this ROI by driving adoption across the organization: focusing on the 20% not the 80%, using automation, planning by initiative, linking variable items to operational activity levels, evaluating "big-bets," making it easy, picking a modern cloud tool, finding an expert, using real-time IoT data, partnering with front-line teams, building early warning systems, and continually improving.

APPLY THE NINE PRINCIPLES

When considering a new forecasting initiative:

Many sponsors (e.g., CFOs, CAOs, CIOs) are experts in their domain but are not experts in creating and deploying modern forecasting. The Nine Principles provide you this expertise. When forecasting uses the Nine Principles, you increase your chance of success.

If you are considering launching a new forecasting initiative, ask yourself how you would apply the Nine Principles. Consider if portions of your existing forecasting processes already adhere to some aspects of the Nine Principles. If so, these could be good starting points to leverage in a revamped process while strengthening your weaker areas.

As you evaluate modern, cloud-based forecasting tools, ask vendors how their products can enable the Nine Principles. As you hire consultants, make sure they understand this is a business project, not an IT project, and you need their help adopting the Principles.

During a forecasting initiative:

When you launch a transformational forecasting initiative, educate your team about the Nine Principles. Print out the Nine Principles and hang them on the wall. Use the Nine Principles to act as your guiding light in the sky.

Explain that this framework ensures everyone's hard work will lead to success. Encourage the team to ask questions like "Is this too detailed?" or "Is this linked to a real-world, operational process?"

Get your executive sponsors and steering committees challenging project requirements if they do not make the process faster, focused on the front lines, real-time, and so on. Ensure decision-makers use the Nine Principles to evaluate requirements, designs, processes, and decisions.

Concluding a forecasting initiative:

The final part of your implementation, before you launch, is to ensure there is a continuous improvement process in place. Your forecasting process is never complete. Your forecasting process needs to live, breathe, and grow more agile, accurate, effective, and faster.

LET THE PRINCIPLES GUIDE YOU!

I developed the Nine Principles from my real-world experiences seeing forecasting projects succeed and sometimes fail. Some get it right, creating dynamic forecasting processes that continuously evolve. Some fail when they miss a crucial element.

The Nine Principles of Agile Planning gives your organization the best chance to build a continuously evolving forecasting process that will succeed. Good luck as you start your voyage creating agile, nimble, and modern forecasting.

Let the Nine Principles guide you!

ABOUT THE AUTHOR

David S. Pabst, CPA/CITP

David is a finance and technology management expert who helps CFOs and Finance organizations create agile, nimble forecasting processes. David started his first software company in high school, and he now uses his expertise in systems, finance, and accounting to create world-class forecasting processes. He advocates for creating simple-to-use, easy-to-understand processes that can be deployed widely throughout an organization with minimal training. David's clients range from Fortune 100 companies to fast-growing start-ups across retail, healthcare, transportation, life sciences, financial services, and manufacturing. David is a frequent speaker and blogger on financial forecasting and reporting topics.

Follow David at twitter.com/datapabst and datapabst.com.

Made in the USA
Las Vegas, NV
24 March 2023